Critters abound around the yard

Ants and flies
to see right here

What are these bugs
you see

Flies and bees don't always please

Where are these creatures from

Not quite the same as once before

Red bugs on red do seem to hide

Butterflies and bees
are friends
of flowers

Different wings
for different things

Butterflies and moths
are different

So very different

Similar are these

So many colors

Friends and neighbors
in a lavender field

Dainty dancers

Butterflies in gracefull flight

Bees for
neighbors

Similar colors

Green can't
hide on red

Many flowers in
Grandma's garden

Yellow
&
orange

Little bug...

big bug

GARDEN PARTY

Moths often look alike

Many kinds of bees like similar flowers

A stone to rest on

One above
three below

No bug
down
here

just a
friendly
flower